This book is dedicated to my children.
Everything is always for you, my loves.

*"We don't inherit the earth
from our ancestors,
we borrow it from our children."*

David Brower

———————————

Laura Tweedale

The joy of
REUSABLE
NAPPIES

A book to help parents thrive
on their cloth nappy journey

Illustrations by Elle Dunn

Bow Bird Press™

First published in 2020 by
Bow Bird Press

Cheshire, England
United Kingdom

Illustrations by Elle Dunn

Published by
Laura Tweedale trading as Bow Bird Press

ISBN 978-1-5272-6803-6

Foreword

In 1839, a German apothecary named Eduard Simon accidentally invented the very first plastic - polystyrene. Over the next 150 years this accident would lead to a revolution in how humans consume across the world.

The first disposable nappies were brought onto the market in the mid-twentieth century, primarily as a product for convenience. (Because washing nappies was more time consuming than throwing them away.) But where once their absorbent cores were made from natural fibres, disposable nappies now contain polymers to keep babies dry, whilst a mix of chemicals will show parents when a nappy is wet, all held together using thermoplastic adhesives.

Unfortunately this so-called convenience comes at a cost: disposable nappies cost parents more in the long run, authorities have to deal with waste costs and it costs our planet too. All that plastic has to go somewhere and now we are seeing the true cost of our reliance on it.

Nearly three billion nappies are being thrown away just in the UK every year. To say we have a problem is an understatement. The Nappy Alliance believes that parents should be given more information about reusable nappies, empowering them to make an informed choice about the products that they choose to use.

As a coalition of independent providers of reusable nappies, the Nappy Alliance exists to promote the economic and environmental benefits of reusable nappies and continues to promote greater consumer choice for parents.

Since 2003 the Nappy Alliance has made significant progress to create a growing market of environmentally friendly products. Now all major supermarkets are stockists and we have seen 30% of parents opting to use them at some stage.

However, the Alliance does not seek a ban on the use of disposable nappies. We fully understand that for many new parents and carers they are a very helpful product and an essential part of managing busy lives. But we believe that governments are right to look at reducing reliance on disposable nappies, along with other single-use plastics, to battle the climate crisis.

As awareness rises over the impact single-use plastics are having on the planet, we have seen more parents begin to make a stand against them. Parents like Laura.

The Joy of Reusable Nappies provides another stepping stone towards making reusable nappies mainstream once again. New parents can rely on Laura's authentic voice and approachable writing to support their journey and dispel the myth that cloth nappies are difficult. (They are not.)

Whether you are considering switching from disposables to reusables, or are expecting your first child and preparing for their arrival, this book will walk you through all you need to know to get going with reusable nappies. Based on the ten biggest questions new parents face when starting out, *The Joy of Reusable Nappies* provides pragmatic and honest advice in a simple, relatable style. Laura offers a practical grounding in the use and care of reusable nappies in a style imbued with optimism and hope: hope of a positive future for the planet and parents everywhere.

Guy Schanschieff MBE
Chair of The Nappy Alliance
nappyalliance.co.uk

Contents

Welcome,
it's so good to have you here

Your curiosity has been piqued. You have
tentatively made that first step to a greener
path to parenthood. You want to use cloth
nappies for your baby, for your journey, for
the love of this planet of ours. I am so glad
you're here.

Hello. I'm Laura, a freelance writer and content creator
from Cheshire, England. I'm a passionate advocate
of living a greener, more sustainable and minimalist
lifestyle. Reusable nappies is one way I share this passion.
I collaborate with a group of parents to create videos for
Instagram TV under the hashtag #clothmadesimple and
share my writing on my website lauratweedale.com. This
book is written from my heart to yours in the knowledge
that living a little greener no longer means you fall into
a stereotype defined by your choice to wear dungarees.

Whether you and your family are city dwellers, off-grid homesteaders, or stand somewhere between the two, I have written this book for you.

MY AUTHORITY

You may be curious as to what my authority over writing about cloth nappies is. The answer may not be what you are expecting. I am not a nappy guru and I have no affiliation to a brand or manufacturer. I do not make or sell them. I am a mother of two children, one who I used cloth nappies with and one I did not. Instead, I offer you a relatable, real life experience, a face and a name and knowledge to take in, rather than a thing to buy (buy buy). I can promise there will be no hard sales here. I won't be telling you which nappies your baby needs, I won't share the brands I have (and love). That's for you and your baby to explore together - oh how joyful a journey it will be.

WHY I CHOSE REUSABLES

Imagine you are facing the ocean. Waves unfurl at your feet as you gently sway to its lulling rhythm. You are rocked left, then right. You are sailing on the open sea, a little boat for one. The rhythm repeats once, twice, again and again until the cadence is lost; until you realise that you can not halt it. You close your eyes to the crashing, the rising, the falling. Nausea creeps upwards. There is no boat. In fact, there is no sand, no sea. But the nausea, it does not cease. Welcome to hyperemesis gravidarum.

I endured that sensation of rocking for the first 30 weeks of pregnancy whilst expecting my son in 2018. The nausea was relentless. For the first 20 weeks my balance was so badly affected I walked with a cane and one day, I fell down the stairs. My daughter was just two years old at the time. I was left with a hypersensitivity to synthetic fragrances so anything in our house with an artificial scent had to go. I started to learn what chemicals lurk in our homes and what impact this has on the world. Hyperemesis was the catalyst that revolutionised my life.

Using cloth with my son has turned out to be a truly gratifying experience. Every single day I know I am doing something that makes my parenting footprint on our Earth a little bit softer. It makes me smile every time I hang nappies on the line to dry in the sunshine. But even more so is that when my children ask me the inevitable question *what did you do to save the world for me?* I can say, hand on my heart: *I tried my best for you, my darlings.*

WHAT YOU CAN EXPECT TO LEARN

In this book I include everything you will want to know, or be questioning, about starting your own cloth nappy journey. It comprises the big ten questions like 'what type of cloth nappy style should I use?' and 'where does the poo go?' There are tips and advice throughout with some truthful tales interspersed from other cloth-using families. I include a checklist for building a thoughtful nappy collection, as well as a handy A - Z of reusable nappy brands and UK-based nappy retailers too.

I have also included a brief overview of the research into the environmental credentials of cloth nappies. I hope the results will surprise, inspire and galvanise you and your decision to choose to reuse.

My aim is that this guide will provide a gentle means of navigation on this reusable nappy journey of yours - a handy pocketbook, there for you in times of need. It is designed to ensure you thrive and so act as a reminder of the unique joy reusable nappies are for you and your baby. I hope it will serve you well.

Take my hand, let's start your wonderful journey together...

I.

What is a reusable nappy?

What is a reusable nappy?

Cloth nappy, real nappy, reusable nappy, natural diaper, washable diaper - there are lots of different terms out there but they all mean the same thing: a nappy you put on your baby that can be used again and again and not sent straight to landfill after a single use. They consist of an absorbing inner part and a waterproof outer part.

They are absolutely marvellous.

TYPES OF MODERN REUSABLE NAPPY
There are four main categories.

» *All-in-one nappy*
» *Pocket nappy*
» *All-in-two / Hybrid nappy*
» *Two-part nappy system*

All-in-one

pocket

Hybrid

Two Part

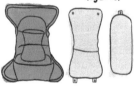
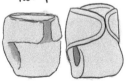

ALL-IN-ONE NAPPY

A nappy that has the outer waterproof shell and the inner absorbent layer attached together as one complete nappy system.

POCKET NAPPY

A nappy that has the outer waterproof shell attached to a lining which has an opening (a pocket) allowing you to choose what type of absorbent insert you would like to use. The insert slides inside the pocket between the outer shell and the lining.

ALL-IN-TWO / HYBRID NAPPY

A nappy that comprises an outer waterproof wrap that comes with multiple absorbent layers that attach by poppers (snaps) inside the shell.

TWO-PART NAPPY SYSTEM

These nappies are typically where most beginner's feel overwhelmed and disheartened. (I blame the word 'system' - it is such an unfriendly term.) I myself was the same. Please don't lose heart. This is the terminology you can expect to read online.

A Two-part nappy system means two separate nappies that are used in conjunction. A separate waterproof outer known as a wrap (often called a shell or cover) must be worn over the top of the absorbent layers. The waterproof outer can be provided by either a wrap made from a polyurethane laminate (PUL) fabric, or a cover made from lanolised wool, sometimes referred to as soakers or longies.

The absorbency can be provided in two ways. The first way is by using a fitted, or shaped nappy. This is a nappy where the entire fabric is absorbent, from front to back, including the sides. This choice allows the outer wrap to be used more than once should it not be soiled. The second way is by folding a fabric square and using a fastening around your baby. Early nappies were made this way. Think back to cloth secured with a large nappy pin. This style can be referred to as a flat lay, prefold or pad nappy. The most commonly thought-of prefold is a 'terry cloth' nappy made from cotton towelling. These flat lay nappies come in a wide variety of fabrics, as do shaped nappies.

SIZING

For All-in-ones, Pockets, Two-parters or All-in-twos / Hybrids, you can buy them in either:
»   *Sized nappies*
»   *Birth to potty*

A 'sized cloth nappy' is appropriate to a baby's weight, a bit like with disposables where they have a guide of what weight range a nappy will fit to.

A 'one size fits most babies' is called a 'Birth to potty' reusable nappy. It has adjusters that shrink or expand the nappy to appropriately fit around your baby's thighs.

These typically fit babies weighing at least eight pounds. For babies weighing eight pounds or less, see 8. 'Can I cloth nappy a newborn?'

WIPES
Whether you choose to use All-in-one, Pocket, Hybrid or Two-part nappies, I urge you to do one thing - choose reusable cloth wipes. I explain why on page 84.

2.

What are inserts, boosters and liners? (Aren't they all the same thing?)

What are inserts, boosters and liners? (Aren't they all the same thing?)

All nappies contain a core that soaks up urine. In most disposable nappies, it's a polymer that absorbs liquid (so called 'eco' nappies have a slightly different make up but do still contain some plastics). In real nappies you can choose either a plant-based, synthetic microfibre, or combination core - this is called an insert.

All-in-one nappies have the insert attached to the shell. For Pocket nappies, you slide your insert(s) of choice into the nappy shell. With a Hybrid or All-in-two, the inserts clip into the wrap. In a Two-part system, your fitted or flat nappy gives the absorbency.

One insert on its own may not be adequate for absorbing

the amount of urine your baby may pass in one movement. You may need to 'boost' it by adding in an extra layer to help soak up the liquid. A booster is simply an extra insert. You can boost all nappy times in one way or another. My Mum told me she used to boost her terry nappies by putting another terry over the top. I am pleased to say things have changed since the 80s.

FABRIC TYPES

There are four fabric types for inserts and boosters. Each have different levels of absorbency. I've ranked the materials from most to least absorbent below:

» *Hemp*
» *Bamboo, or combined bamboo and charcoal*
» *Cotton, or organic cotton*
» *Synthetic Microfibre (commonly a polyester or polyamide)*
» *A combination of two or more of all of the above*

The more absorbent an insert is, the longer it will take to dry. Microfibres are an excellent, quick-drying material, but made from polyester (commonly made from petroleum oil or 'crude' oil). Hemp is brilliant for boosting a night time nappy that may be worn for up to 12 hours, but slow to dry after laundering. A variety of each will stand you in good stead. I have one, or two, of each type.

WHY LINE YOUR NAPPIES

A liner is placed inside your cloth nappy and sits against

baby's skin. It's main purpose is to catch any bowel movements, making your nappies easier to clean. Some have the additional benefit of wicking moisture away from baby's skin so they remain dry to the touch.

CHOICE OF LINER
There are two types of liners - disposable or reusable.

Disposable liners
These are made from paper, bamboo, cellulose or viscose. Some are marketed as compostable, but you should not put a soiled nappy into a household compost bin. This is because home / small scale composters do not reach high enough temperatures to kill off any pathogens or bacteria that may be found in human excreta, which can spread disease. It is also not recommended liners be flushed in the toilet. A conundrum of how to safely dispose of them, for sure.

Reusable liners
These are made from fleece, polyester, bamboo or even silk. For soiled liners, they can be lifted out of a nappy and the contents easily disposed of into the toilet. Whether wet or soiled, reusable liners can be washed with all your nappies and reused again and again. No waste. They are my preference. I made mine from an old fleece blanket and the polyester fabric cover that came with my shaped changing mat when I could no longer use the mat because my son was able to sit up. They really needn't cost the earth.

3.

How do I fit a reusable nappy? (and do they leak?)

How do I fit a reusable nappy? (and do they leak?)

Both sized nappies and birth-to-potty nappies are adjustable at the waist. They can either have a Velcro fastening or have 'snaps', or poppers as we say in the UK.

FASTENINGS AND RISE SNAPS

For birth-to-potty nappies, you change the fit by adjusting the 'rise snaps.' These are two or three rows of poppers on the front of the nappy that allow you to shorten the nappy's length, therefore reducing the size of the leg holes. Chances are, the first time you look at an adjustable cloth nappy and see thirty 'snaps' all over its front, your head may reel.

I liken it to the first time you try to popper up a sleepsuit on your baby - the snaps around the crotch are confusing at first, but a breeze after your tenth (hundredth) change. In time, you won't even notice the rise snaps are there.

OH MY THEY LOOK GOOD

Cloth nappies and disposable nappies look different on a baby. If you have started out with disposables, or, like me, decided to make the switch to reusables after your first child (children) you may be startled by how different a cloth nappy looks on your baby compared to a disposable.

Disposables fit high on the waist, sometimes reaching as far up as baby's belly button. Cloth nappies tend to look more like they are going to hang off their bottom. This was tricky for me, having used (5,475) disposables with my daughter for two and a half years, and then choosing cloth nappies for my son. Reusable nappies fit right across the hip bone, usually where a crease between the pelvis and the stomach can be found. They happen to be very beautiful looking too.

GETTING THE FIT RIGHT

All babies are unique, which is essentially why there are so many varieties of modern cloth nappy out there. What fits well on one child may not be quite right on another. Velcro may suit your baby better than one that closes with poppers. A double gusset on the leg may sit just right during the day when your little one is off exploring the world, but a single leg gusset may give that looser fit you prefer for restful nights.

PUTTING A CLOTH NAPPY ON YOUR BABY

The back of the nappy should sit at the top of baby's bottom. Pull the front of the nappy up between baby's legs until the waistband lays across the hip bones. It should be parallel to the back of the nappy. Take one back wing and pull it at a slight upwards angle over the hip to meet the fastenings at the front. Doing this upward motion, rather than simply flipping the wing at 90 degrees, will help give a snug fit across the hip. Fasten and repeat on the opposite side.

FASTENING A NAPPY

A common mistake when starting out with reusable nappies is to fasten them too tightly around baby's tummy. That is because when baby is lying down, their tummy is depressed, but as soon as they sit up, their tummy compresses and needs a bit more room to have the space to sit comfortably. Once your nappy is fastened, make sure you can easily slide two fingers between baby's tummy and the nappy's waistband. If you find that this is a squeeze, simply loosen the fastening.

If you are using a nappy that has rise fasteners, you should adjust this before you secure the side fastenings. If you notice that the front of baby's nappy sits higher up at the front than at the back, it may be that the rise fasteners are set too wide and therefore makes your nappy loose. It is much easier to undo the side fastenings and readjust the rise than to try and adjust the rise whilst baby is still wearing the nappy - in my experience.

FIT TIP

Sometimes a nappy can fit baby between the rise settings. For a small adjustment, try tucking the folded fabric from between the rise fastenings up towards the waistband for a slightly snugger fit, or down towards the crotch for a looser fit.

FINAL CHECKS

You've popped a clean nappy on baby. My, it looks good. Check that the leg gussets are tucked into baby's natural knicker line (not straight across the thigh) and that you can comfortably fit two fingers around the elastics here as well. Check that no absorbent inserts or liners have gone rouge and are peeping over your waterproof layer. Run your finger around the leg cuff and check the elastics haven't rolled out so the lining is visible. If it has, simply tuck it back in until you only see the waterproof PUL wrap or wool soaker around those delicious, chubby baby legs. Yum, yum, yum.

FAT NAPPIES

A disposable nappy and a reusable nappy, whichever style of cloth you choose, are a very different thickness. Disposables, especially when first put on, are only a few millimetres thick (until they absorb urine, or water as I have seen in a public swimming pool before). A reusable nappy leans more towards centimetres in thickness, depending on how many boosters you use.

Sadly, many high street children's clothing retailers

have not caught up with the growing demand of clothes designed to fit a cloth bottom... yet.

DRESSING A CLOTH BUM

There are some fabulous brands out there making trousers, dungarees, shorts, leggings, tights, palazzo-style pants for cloth nappied babies but you may have to rely on buying online. Or, as is my go-to for my son's clothing, I put him in a larger size than his age. Lots of trousers have elastic adjusters inside the waistband to ensure a good fit across the waist. A trouser's leg length can be altered by simply folding up, or cutting off any excess and using an iron-on hemming tape, if you're not au fait with sewing. Buying second hand children's clothing from preloved markets and online auction sites can provide affordable options too.

IT'S U, NOT V

When choosing trousers or leggings for your cloth nappy baby, look at the shape of the inner leg seam. A more comfortable shape to fit over a reusable nappy is a trouser with a curved inner seam, shaped more like an upside down U, than those that meet in a narrow, triangular shaped point at the centre of the crotch.

MY NAPPIES LEAK. WHAT'S WRONG?

Firstly, don't be despondent. As your baby grows, starts to crawl, takes those first tentative steps, and then those great strides out into this wonderful world of ours, their bodies change, their needs change and so do their nappies. You may have to add in extra absorbency, or lengthen the nappy if it's an All-in-one. It may be that the style of nappy you're using isn't suitable for the occasion. I used a sling to carry my son and would regularly suffer from a 'compression' leak.

Think of the absorbent insert as a sponge, soaking up all the urine and holding it in its fibres. Just like with any other type of sponge, give it a squeeze and what happens? The liquid runs out. The weight of my son pressing down on the nappy in the sling was enough to ring out the liquid. I quickly learnt which nappies suited those occasions better.

Other common reasons a nappy may leak include:
» *A nappy has reached saturation point* - it simply can't hold any more contents
» *A nappy is being flooded* - the amount of urine being released is a greater volume than the absorbent layer is able to soak up quickly enough
» (or, surprisingly commonly) *a nappy isn't on quite right.* My husband's been known to put the outer wrap on back to front, or inside out. I've fallen foul of the absorbent insert poking out the pocket, allowing my son's clothes to wick urine up his back! However, I have also accidentally ripped the Velcro tabs off a fair few disposable nappies, rendering them useless and having to throw them away without a single use. Mistakes happen. We're human after all.

VEST EXTENDERS

Popper-fastening vests and bodysuits are common clothing items for babies up until they're ready to be potty trained. Often these will be too small in the crotch to go around a reusable nappy but sizing up leaves the vest slipping off baby's shoulders. You need a vest extender. They are a game changer. A vest extender is a small piece of fabric with snaps on either edge that allow a popper-closing vest or bodysuit to be extended over a cloth nappy without distorting the vest's neckline. They also help ensure you're not squeezing a nappy with clothing that is too tight, which may result in leaks.

Remember...

* *If you plan to sell your nappies, use liners to help mitigate potential stains.*
* *Ensure you can comfortably fit two fingers between baby's tummy and the nappy waistband.*
* *Look for leggings or trousers that curve like an upside down 'u' in the inner leg seam and crotch for a loose fit over a cloth bum.*
* *Keep a spare vest extender in your changing bag. (You can thank me later.)*

4.

Where do I store dirty nappies?

Where do I store dirty nappies?

There are two types of storage you may choose to use, either a wet bag or a nappy bucket. Both methods mean you do not have to touch dirty nappies to load them into your washing machine.

WET BAG

A wet bag is made of the same waterproof fabric as the waterproof shell on real nappies (it's usually PUL - a polyester/polyurethane laminated knit fabric). Wet bags usually have a handy hanging tab for keeping out of reach of little fingers, and are what you would take with you when cloth nappying out of your home. The wet bag can be unzipped and it, along with all its contents, can go in the washing machine altogether.

NAPPY BUCKET

A nappy bucket or nappy pail is a bucket with a secure

lid (not rocket science). Any bucket with a lid will work, but I use a branded nappy bucket that has handy internal hooks. The hooks allow me to hang a mesh laundry bag inside so I can lift the whole bag and all the dirty nappies out in one go and pop them inside my washing machine without having to handle dirty nappies.

CLOSE THE LAUNDRY TABS

If you use nappies with Velcro fastenings you will see that there is a strip of soft looped Velcro inside the nappy. This allows you to fold the hooked Velcro back on itself so it attaches to the looped Velcro inside, without refastening the nappy like you would on your baby. The nappy needs to be 'open' when it is being washed. Not closing the laundry tabs can result in balding of material or damage to the Velcro - I am forever getting cloth wipes stuck to mine because I rush and don't close the tabs properly. If this happens and your Velcro becomes congested by lint, tweezers or short fingernails work a treat at removing any fluff.

NAPPIES ARE FOR REAL LIFE, NOT JUST FOR INSTAGRAM

Lengthen the life of your Velcro by not opening the laundry tabs and refastening across the waistband after washing just because it 'looks neat'. This is causing unnecessary wear and tear to your nappies, despite how many beautiful photos on social media may say otherwise. Leave the nappy wings free to fly. They will thank you for their freedom in the long run.

TO SOAK OR NOT TO SOAK

When my mother used cloth nappies on my sister and I, all terry nappies went into a bucket full of a nappy sterilising liquid and soaked for a number of days until she was ready to do a wash. I have never soaked any of my modern cloth nappies. You see, if you were to compare a washing machine from the 1980s with one from 2020, I can imagine the differences far outweigh the similarities. Developments in washing technology, detergents and the fabrics of today's reusable nappies are vastly disparate. A well sealed wet bag or securely fitting lid on a nappy bucket keeps any unwanted smells at bay until you have enough to fill a load.

Please be aware prolonged contact with water can damage some fabrics. If you are considering soaking your nappies, check the manufacturer's guidelines to see if it is suitable.

5.

How do I wash reusable nappies?

(And where does the poo go?)

How do I
wash reusable nappies?
(And where does the poo go?)

The plethora of information online would have you believe that caring for your real nappies is as difficult as caring for your baby. Oh how complicated we make this world of ours. There are three things you need to know when it comes to washing your nappies. Rinse, wash, use a powder detergent. Wow, that was easy, right?

RINSE

When you load your dirty nappies into your machine, first you will need to run a rinse cycle, or 'pre-wash.' This will help to break down the ammonia in the inserts and start to break down any solids or stains. You can reduce your spin speed on your machine. I do mine at 800. This can help preserve any leg elastics.

WASH

When I started my real nappy journey, I searched and searched to find someone to talk to about what to do. I found a cloth nappy library (see page 70) in the county that borders mine. I would have to drive forty minutes to have a chat. (Not very eco, I agree.) My daughter went to preschool for the day and I packed up my son and drove all the way to meet Jo, who ran the library. Her words hang in the air every time I load my washing machine: *Press every button.*

Modern washing machines are designed to reduce water usage, so an 'average' washing cycle, perhaps the daily mode you might ordinarily use, won't fill the drum with enough water to flush out a cloth nappy's contents. You need to 'press every button' so you have a long enough cycle to ensure you have an adequate amount of water to thoroughly clean your nappies. I select the 'cottons' setting, washing at 60 degrees. On my machine, after a little trial and error, it turned out I need only press one button - the Intensive Wash function. This cycle lasts two hours 35 minutes. As the programme comes to an end, there are no visible detergent suds in my machine. This is the goal.

POWDER, NO SOFTENER

I am no chemist, but if you read the back of your liquid laundry detergent or fabric softener bottles you will find they both contain this - Cationic Surfactants. This is what keeps clothes soft. It binds to the fabric until it is rubbed off by daily wear, or is broken down by detergent and washed away. They have a positive charge which makes them hydrophobic - they repel water. Not what you want your cloth nappies to do. Over time, cationic surfactants can build up to a level that means your absorbent inserts can no longer soak up liquid. They are a no-no for washing your cloth nappies. Most liquid detergents also contain cationic surfactants, whilst powdered detergents do not. They have the opposite - Anionic Surfactants. These have a negative charge which makes them hydrophilic - they just love water. So back to good old fashioned powders we go, usually in a beautiful, plastic-free, recyclable cardboard box. Tick, tick, tick.

BIOLOGICAL VERSES NON BIOLOGICAL

It's all about enzymes. An enzyme is a protein. They regulate the speed in which a chemical reaction happens. Essentially, they degrade materials. The enzymes in biological laundry detergent have been specifically chosen because of their abilities to breakdown organic matters commonly found on our soiled fabrics, particularly fat and grease. These enzymes are not included in non biological detergents. Historically, these enzymes have been blamed as causes for skin irritation, allergic reaction or uticaria (hives). In 2008 Dr David Basketter and colleagues from St Thomas' Hospital, Nottingham University and St Mary's Hospital[1] conducted a piece of

1 NHS (2008). *Bio washing powder rashes a 'myth'.* Available from
www.nhs.uk/news/lifestyle-and-exercise/bio-washing-powder-rashes-a-myth/
[Accessed 10 July 2020].

research into this theory. It was concluded that enzymes in biological laundry detergents were not responsible for causing the above concerns.

You may be surprised to learn that there are only a handful of countries across the world that manufacture non biological laundry detergent. For the majority of municipalities, their detergents contain enzymes and there is no enzyme-free alternative.

Enzymes may be listed in the ingredients of a biological detergent but not whether the enzymes contain cellulase. Cellulases break down cellulose - the main building block of plant cells. If you have natural fibre nappies, the cellulase will happily break down, in equal measure, any cellulose found in a soiled nappy, as well as the nappy fibres itself. As an example, the cellulose content of cotton fibre is 90%. This is why you may be advised not to use biological detergents with natural fibre nappies because we are not told what enzymes are being used. You would need to contact the detergent manufacturer to ask if cellulase is used.

The choice to use biological or non biological is your own. Some nappy brands offer a warranty on their products which they void if their nappies have been washed using biological detergents. So it is best to check this before making your decision. Again, I am not a chemist, so I urge you to do some research of your own.

WHERE DOES THE POO GO?

I've tried my utmost to be factual here, but not graphic.
If you are expecting your first child, the following
information may seem somewhat distasteful, but I
can promise you, from my heart to yours, that dealing
with your child's bodily fluids will quickly become
so normalised that you won't even give this a second
thought. Trust me.

When your child begins potty training, where would
their poo go? In fact, where does yours go? The notion of
emptying a soiled nappy into a toilet seems alien in our
modern culture, even though we would never consider
sending an older child's or adult's faeces to landfill or for
incineration. Of course a baby's bowel movements, until
weaned, are vastly different to that of a solid-food eating
human. And that is the crux of this issue. Until your baby
is passing solid stools, or ones that contain undigested
food, your soiled nappies can be washed in your washing
machine. Breast or bottle fed, a pre-weaned baby's faecal
matter is water soluble, can pass through the filters in
modern washing machines and be processed along with
all our other household waste water.

For weaned babies, there are typically two ways of
emptying poo from a nappy. With a solid stool, this
can simply be tipped into the toilet and flushed away.
With a loose stool, for example when teething, you will
need to remove all the solid, semi-solid or semi-liquid
contents before it goes into your machine. The easiest

way typically is to 'sluice' - hold the liner or nappy in the toilet bowl under the water outlet and flush. When sluicing, be mindful of the force of your toilet's flush. (I've lost a liner this way since my high-rise cistern is somewhat overzealous!)

Alternatively you may prefer to remove the contents using toilet paper or a tool to scrape the contents from the nappy. I have an old, blunt knife, stored in a secure box in my WC for such eventualities. (I have heard others prefer a spatula).

WON'T THERE BE POO IN MY WASHING MACHINE?

After you've washed a pair of muddy trousers, greasy tea towels, smelly workout clothes, do you open your machine and go oh, what a mess? No. Your clothes and your washing machine are clean. The only time there could be a problem is if you do not empty the contents of a soiled nappy before you put it in the machine. We all have bowel movements that can contain undigested food, your weaned baby is no different. This can block your washing machine filter in the same way a rogue hair clip or piece of loose change can. The poo goes in the loo before it goes in your machine. It really is that simple.

Inevitably, and very sadly, this is the issue that hinders many cloth nappy journeys. It would be remiss not to address that sluicing nappies is one of my least favourite parenting jobs. I also find the worry over my children, their health and development, if they're happy and how I keep them safe in this tumultuous world are also things I'd prefer a lesser dose of too. But I am their mother and if dealing with a little bit of poo and a lot of worry gives me such rich rewards, I will do it. And my goodness, it is worth it.

MY NAPPIES DO NOT FILL MY MACHINE

If you have a large drum machine, you may be concerned that you don't have enough dirty nappies to justify washing a small load. After the initial rinse cycle, why not bulk out the load with other items that can be washed at the same temperature as your nappies? Just be sure to check the washing instructions of those other items carefully... my 100% wool jumper got mixed in with some towels recently and it came out too small for even my one year old to get his arms through.

EMOLLIENTS AND NAPPY RASH CREAMS

'Cloth nappy wearing babies don't get nappy rash...' is something you may be told when you start your reusable nappy journey. That, and *'you can not use a nappy cream when you use real nappies.'* Please, do not be disheartened if your baby develops a sore bottom. Every baby is different, eats different foods, has different milks, cuts teeth differently. Not all babies may have nappy rash. Both of my children did.

The reason you will be advised against any type of emollient is that they can be hard to breakdown by detergents and therefore affect the absorbency of your nappies. Should you need a cream, there are two things you can do to help. Firstly, use a liner. This acts as a barrier between the nappy's lining and baby's skin, which can help keep the emollient where it needs to be. Secondly, opt for a cream with natural ingredients. I've found that any emollient that turns transparent on application works very well. If you are unsure if it is nappy rash, speak to your healthcare professional.

STRIP WASHING

All babies eat a different diet. All washing machines vary. Water quality changes from town to town. These factors mean you will not find a 'one size fits all' for washing your nappies. It takes a little figuring out. A few attempts and I was sorted. My wash routine was successful, it remains unchanged for over a year. Then I used someone else's machine.

We enjoyed a long weekend away, I didn't think twice about taking my cloth nappies to wash in a machine other than my own. The machine's owner was fine about it. I did everything I would normally do at home. The cycle finished. They were rancid. To this day I can not be certain what it was that affected my nappies. I'd used my own detergent, run a programme as close to the one I run on my own machine. But something had gone very wrong. They smelt of wet dog and they stank even when they were dry. There was only one thing left to do - it was time to 'strip wash'.

A strip wash is a way of ensuring there is no detergent or barrier cream residue blocking your nappies' abilities to absorb liquid. If your nappies one day start giving off a distinct odour (often caused by a build of ammonia), or you find they can not hold their usual volume of urine, you may need to do the same. Run your wash the same as you would ordinarily. Then you have a choice. Either, run your cycle again without any detergent. Alternatively, run multiple rinse cycles until there are no visible suds when your nappies are rinsing out. This is all I have ever done. An often sweared-by strip washing technique commonly suggested in the cloth nappy community is to leave your nappies out in a good old downpour. The pH balance of rain is said to neutralise any build up of detergents and, provided they have a thorough soaking, should rinse out any stubborn detergent residue.

DRYING NAPPIES

PUL nappies cannot be tumble dried as the heat can melt the coating that makes them waterproof. However, some natural fibre nappies are safe to tumble - check the brand's care instructions first. If you have nappies that can be tumble dried, there is a way you can reduce your drying time (and therefore your energy consumption). Wool dryer balls. All natural, non synthetic, chemical free dryer balls help to speed up the drying time and keep fabrics soft. They are also much quieter than those plastic

dryer balls - perfect for when baby is (finally) asleep.
Line drying nappies is the most cost effective way of
drying cloth nappies but sadly, we do not all live in places
with beautifully clement weather 365 days of the year.
Be aware that PUL can be damaged by direct heat. If you
line dry, face the PUL away from the sun when you hang
them out and bring them in as soon as they are dry, if you
can. Never put a PUL nappy directly on a radiator or else
it may melt. If you are air drying your nappies indoors,
remember that heat rises. Try hanging those slow drying
bamboo or cotton nappies at the top of your airer where
there is better airflow and warmer climes.

REMOVING STAINS

You will never find a better, more natural stain remover
than the sun. Get those nappies in the fresh air, or hang
them in a sunny window. It is the only remover I have
ever used. An octopus style hanging clothes airer (the one
with the pegs attached) can be your best friend here.

TIP TOP WASH

Your washing machine is working the hardest it may ever
have had to before. Treat it to some TLC. Run a cleaning
cycle regularly. I do mine every six weeks. I run the empty
machine on a 60 degree wash, no detergent, just an egg
cup full of bicarbonate of soda to help prevent a build up
of limescale (which is not a friend).

6.

Can I use cloth nappies outside of the house?

If so, how?

Can I use cloth nappies outside of the house?

If so, how?

REUSABLES ON HOLIDAY
When writer and cloth nappy parent Emma Reed (emmareed.net) and her family visited Florida from the UK, it never occurred to her not to take her one year old son's cloth nappies too.

"William had been in reusable nappies since he was six months old, after we'd navigated the experience of having a baby prematurely. Six months later, I was packing almost every cloth nappy I owned into a small, hand luggage sized suitcase ready for two weeks in Florida. We use cloth nappies, I didn't see why that would change just because we were away from home.

On the plane, I had full access to everything I needed for changing his nappy in the small suitcase. Even though the flight was nine hours, honestly it was easy. The dirty ones went inside a wetbag and kept away from the clean ones. Plus I had plenty to see us through the journey.

We had two holiday homes over our two week stay and both came fully equipped with washing machines. I followed the same wash routine as I do at home. Before we were due to leave, I did a wash of all of his nappies and wipes (and our clothes too!) It meant that I wouldn't have all of that laundry to do back at home and that I would have clean nappies for the flight.

So many people seem to find using cloth nappies outside of the house daunting and scary. I hope my experience proves it really isn't."

CLOTH AND CHILDCARE SETTINGS

In the UK, it is an offence for nappies to be included in general waste on a commercial premises. It is also law that a business offering baby changing facilities as a public convenience must provide dedicated nappy bins. It costs businesses vast amounts of money (and time) to dispose of nappies appropriately. Talk to your childcare provider first. They may be dab-hands at changing a real nappy, or (hopefully) they may be willing to learn. Discuss the best method for storing dirty nappies. Wetbags are usually best here.

As you now know, there are four types of cloth nappy. Some of these may be more suited to a childcare setting than others. All-in-ones may be preferable for nurseries whereas a childminder with only a few charges may be more than happy to use Two-part nappies.

In a nursery environment, you should be prepared to receive back any of your child's soiled nappies which still include some of the nappy's contents. After all, they are responsible for a number of children and they need to reduce the time anything takes their attention away from their charges (like sluicing a nappy soiled by a loose stool). I would rather have a dirty nappy returned to me and my child have their full attention in the moment, wouldn't you? You may therefore prefer to use a disposable liner for childcare days. Remember to remind your caregiver that disposable liners should be disposed of in a bin rather than flushing down a toilet - a blocked toilet in a nursery would have far greater consequences than one in your own home.

You will need to ensure your childcare provider has enough nappies and wetbags to see them through each day. Make sure your nappies are 'stacked' - that they have the appropriate inserts and liners layered inside each nappy and folded so they are easy to handle. This is your responsibility, not theirs, so do this the night before. When I was working in the city, I had to leave the house with my daughter by 7:15am. If my bag wasn't packed the night before, it set me up to fail that day.

DAYS OUT

I've not taken my son over the Atlantic ocean like Emma, but I do cloth nappy my son out and about every day. I have had curious questions from other parents who have never seen a reusable nappy before. Not once has someone reacted negatively. The first few trips out I was undeniably nervous. I had used disposables for my daughter for two and a half years, now I had two children and real nappies on my hands. Could I do this? Of course I could, that's why I've written this book for you. Before long, like me, you won't give it a second thought.

REUSABLE SWIM NAPPIES

The very first time I took my daughter swimming, I was prepared. I had both my disposable swimming nappy and the separate neoprene cover, also known as a 'Happy Nappy' or 'Jammers', packed in our swim bag. Before I was about to leave, my baby girl needed her nappy changing. *It's only ten minutes up the road*, I thought to myself. I'll pop her disposable nappy on now and then put the cover on over the top when we get there. What I did not know is that disposable swimming nappies are not absorbent at all. She, the car seat (and me by the time I realised what had happened,) were soaked through. So what is the point of using a disposable swimming nappy compared to a reusable one? Like with any other nappy, it is all about what to do with poo.

The neoprene cover is there for one reason - containment. The nappy is there for one reason - to make it easier to clean up any solids should baby have a bowel movement in the pool. Neither a disposable swim nappy nor a reusable swim nappy absorb liquid. If they did, your poor child would be dragging around half the pool's water contents whilst they try to splash.

There are a number of reusable swimming nappies on the market. Different styles offer different changing practicalities. You know your child and your swimming pool's facilities best. If you don't, then I encourage you to go and find out. There is nothing more joyful than seeing your little one be happy and safe in the water.

Remember...

* *Wet bags are excellent space savers and can be hung up high, away from little 'explorers'.*
* *Nappy buckets with mesh laundry bags inside mean you do not have to handle soiled nappies.*
* *Biological detergent can degrade natural fibres.*
* *Use a powder detergent, no fabric softener at all.*
* *Pack your changing bag the night before for an easier morning departure.*

7.

Can I use cloth nappies
at night?

Can I use
cloth nappies at night?

The short answer: Absolutely.

The long answer: Absolutely, but be prepared for a little bit of trial and error and be mindful that babies grow!

Once baby stops night feeds, or is of an age where you no longer want to disturb their sleep by changing their nappy in the night, you will need to increase the amount of absorbency your nappy can offer. Most modern reusables advise you to change the nappy every three hours. At night, a baby can sleep for up to twelve hours. That's a big jump. Where does the extra absorbency to stretch another nine hours come from?

GETTING THROUGH THE NIGHT
My son was born weighing ten pounds two and a half ounces and was the 99th centile for length. By six months

he was the same weight as my daughter when she turned one year old. The nappies that should have lasted him through the night for his age were never going to work. At eleven months of age, he was still feeding three times during the night. (That was a difficult time.) His nappies were at saturation every four to six hours, if I didn't change him. This is the point where I almost gave up on cloth nappies. It turned out all I needed to do was ask for help.

HELP AT HAND

I had relied on birth-to-potty All-in-ones and Pocket nappies for my son in the beginning, thinking I needn't dip my toe into the sized nappy / Two-part nappy market. (Shopping often leaves me overwhelmed and indecisive.) I supposedly thought I had all I needed. I was wrong. And that's the thing about babies, they change and grow and so do their needs. I just wasn't quick enough to realise that.

After one disasterous night where I was sleep deprived and set to resign, I messaged my friend Amy and said there is no way I can get a nappy to work at night time. She, along with some other cloth nappy friends, pointed me in the direction of a particular combination they thought would work. A bamboo fitted nappy with a booster between the nappy and the wrap. I have not changed my night time Two-part combination for six months. I wonder if I ever will.

Some of my friends' children can go through the night in a simple Pocket nappy with one good insert, no booster required. My son couldn't (still can not). Every child is unique. Know your baby and ask for help if you need it.

8.

Are reusable nappies suitable
for a newborn baby?

Are reusable nappies suitable for a newborn baby?

My daughter was born at seven pounds five ounces on a snowy new year's eve. Four hours after she arrived in this world she was admitted to the Neonatal Special Care Unit with suspected meningitis. It was one of the most difficult moments of my life. Despite this, I still regret not having used cloth nappies with her.

When I was expecting my son, I suffered from hyperemesis gravidarum - a severe form of nausea and vomiting during pregnancy. I knew I wanted to try reusables with him but frankly, I was too sick to learn before he arrived. I regret missing out on the experience of using cloth nappies with a newborn, but at the time I was consumed with trying to survive.

WHAT TO CHOOSE

Welcoming a newborn safely into the world, whether they are your first or fifth child, is a heady, dreamlike time. Using cloth from birth can of course be done but many families choose to wait a few weeks. (Parents need looking after during this fourth trimester too.) The most crucial thing to consider is a nappy system that both you and your partner agree to use. My husband has a preference for Velcro fastenings. I don't really mind. Having to hunt around the clean laundry to make sure the ones you or she/he/they prefer is something no new parent has time to do.

WELCOME LITTLE ONE

Amy Whitehead, Stone Conservator and writer of clothmadesimple.com began her cloth nappy journey when she returned home from bringing her son Gilbert safely into the world. He was just five days old.

"We had been given a selection of preloved All-in-two nappy systems in birth-to-potty sizes so it made sense to use the ones we had been gifted first. Gilbert was six pounds when he was born and in hindsight, the Birth-to-potty sizes were too big for our petite baby. Nevertheless, they worked. We then decided to add some newborn wraps to our collection. With the sheer volume of nappies used in the beginning, we found folded muslins were quick drying and had the added benefit of being far less bulky on our little boy."

PREFOLDS

Prefolds are the most economic, flexible reusable nappy out there. They can be folded in numerous ways. They come in a variety of fabrics such as cotton terry towelling, or light muslin cloth, and can be adjusted according to your baby's size. It is all in how you fold them. They also dry quickly. You can expect to change your newborn's nappy every two to three hours, including at night. That's upward of twelve nappy changes in 24 hours. If you don't run a wash and dry them every day, you can see how many nappies you will need. A pack of 12 terry nappies can cost around £25 ($31). There are some All-in-one nappies on the market at the same price point for a single nappy.

FOLDING A FLAT OR PREFOLD

Perhaps the most traditional fold out there is the Kite Fold. My mother can still remember how to do this thirty odd years later (I've watched her, it's a marvel). But long gone are the large nappy pins used to secure these folded nappies. Modern fasteners, or 'nippas' are now on the market too.

Square, Kite, Bat, Triangle, Jo or Tri-Fold, there are a wide variety of folding styles to explore with your little one, too many to include every adaptation in this book. Instead I have chosen the simplest and most commonly used, which you will find a plethora of excellent video tutorials for online. You may even enjoy coming up with new versions of your own. No matter how many folding

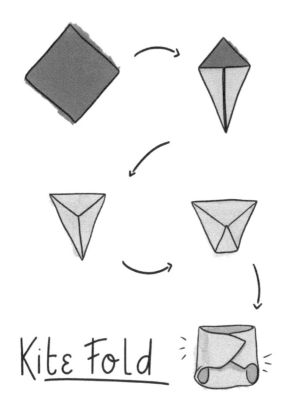

Kite Fold

Tri-Fold

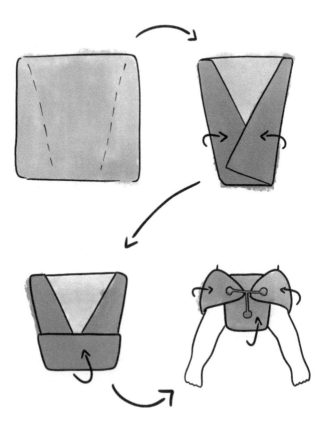

methods there are to experiment with now, each can be a simple pleasure to do. There is nothing quite as soothing for the soul as folding nappies.

PREMATURE BABIES AND CLOTH NAPPIES

When my daughter was admitted to the Neonatal Special Care Unit a handful of hours after her birth, my eyes were opened to the desperate challenges families with premature babies face. My girl, all seven pounds five ounces of her, appeared a giant compared to the tiny five pound premature babies in the neighbouring incubators. Side by side, we parents chatted and hummed and took care of our babies, but the one thing that will never leave me was the experience of having to change my newborn's first nappies through the arm holes of an incubator. That is something I wish for no parent.

There are reusable nappies available specifically catering to newborns, typically with a weight range starting at six or seven pounds, fitting up to around twelve pounds. However there is another option you can consider. Whilst in Special Care with my daughter I will never forget the moment I watched a father, whose baby was also in the unit, take up a pair of scissors and trim his baby's disposable nappy down to size. Inspired yet heartbreaking in equal measure. You could consider doing the same with a muslin or flat nappy, therefore creating a bespoke nappy for your beautiful, unique baby.

9.

How many reusable nappies do I really need to have to go 'full time'?

How many reusable nappies do I really need to have to go 'full time'?

When I visited the cloth nappy library, the organiser was quite forthright - fifteen for day, five for night, at a minimum.

This was an excellent place to start and so I suggest you do the same. With time comes a better understanding of you and your baby's needs. There is more than a number to consider.

WHAT TO CONSIDER

If you search online 'how many cloth nappies do I need?' you will get results ranging from ten to forty. The two factors I urge you to consider is how many times a week you want to be washing nappies, and how long will you be prepared to wait for them to dry. If you are going to line or air dry all your inserts, be mindful of how long this can be. Hemp and bamboo can take up to 48 hours.

If you will be using childcare outside of your home, I would consider increasing the size of your collection so the nursery can keep some spares to hand. I keep three nappies in my changing bag at all times and have enough to stop me from dipping into it whilst I am home. This means I am less likely to be caught short without a spare nappy when changing out of the house.

I have 22 nappies for daytime and five for night. I wash every other day. This suits me perfectly (but I have yet to fall foul of covetting specific prints, a common side effect of joining the reusable nappy community.). Don't get hung up on finding the perfect number of nappies - you, your baby and your circumstances all factor into what makes ten, twenty, or thirty+ right for you.

BUILDING A THOUGHTFUL NAPPY COLLECTION

I hate the term 'stash'. It's common amongst the real nappy community to refer to your collection in this term. But I am crossing it out here. Stash sounds like an abundance of nappies hoarded with greed. As a minimalist, I simply don't like it. The word feels wrong in my mouth. With thoughtfulness and some patience, you can create a collection without the need for others to covet. The best way to begin is to try before you buy.

REAL NAPPY VOUCHER SCHEMES

In 2020 there were 41 local authorities across the UK offering vouchers to support parents to buy their own cloth nappies. Eight of those councils are in London alone. Councils incur huge costs in managing the safe disposal of single use nappies. They have got wise to the need for change. My local authority partners with a nappy brand and sent me two Birth-to-potty nappies free of charge, along with a selection of liners. Other councils are refunding parents on proof of receipt for real nappies, up to as much as £54 in north London.

The easiest way to check if your council offers an incentive is to simply search for the term 'real nappies incentive' on their website. This is how I found my scheme. If they don't, why not consider writing to them or coveting your local MP and asking for them to start a scheme. (Go on, call them out for being oh so behind the times.)

If you are in London, go to realnappiesforlondon.org.uk

USING A NAPPY LIBRARY
It is without a doubt that had I not made the journey to meet a fellow cloth nappy mum at a nappy library almost twenty miles from my home, this book may never have been written. Her no-nonsense approach was the voice I longed to hear. I hope mine is serving you in the same way across these pages.

Nappy libraries work pretty much in the same way as other libraries all over the world, except they often require a deposit and suggest a donation to help with their running costs (like washing or buying nappies). You hire a kit that typically comprises multiple versions of every type of nappy, along with accessories and notes for guidance on how to care for the nappies in this collection. Each library will set their own structure for payments. As an example, I borrowed over 50 nappies for a donation of £10 a month with a returnable £20 deposit. The library also had close links with a range of nappy manufacturers and were able to offer discounts on some brands too. All you have to do is remember to ask.

To find a nappy library in your area in the UK, go to uknappynetwork.org

HIRING NAPPIES

If there is no nappy library in your local area, a hiring scheme may be more appropriate. These are complete kits you rent for a period of time, usually paying a fee and leaving a (sometimes large) deposit with the rental company. These book up quickly and can have long waiting lists. If you wish to hire for your newborn, put your name on a list six months in advance.

LAUNDRY SERVICES

When my parents were children in the fifties, a nappy laundry service was as common as toasters are today. With less and less families using cloth nappies, their numbers have sadly waned. If you would prefer to pay for your nappies to be taken away and returned clean to you, then consider a nappy laundry service. Check their terms and conditions before signing up - it would be fruitless to use a laundry service that can only wash the two flat nappies you have in your collection.

If you are in the UK you can try contacting your local National Childbirth Trust (NCT) branch for a list of laundry services available.

Find your local NCT group at nct.org.uk

Remember...

* *A selection of all types will see you
  right throughout your journey.*
* *The level of absorbency you need will vary
  with your child's age, weight, diet and activity.*
* *Natural fibres are slow to dry but offer the highest
  absorbency. They are especially good for sleeping
  and sling-wearing.*
* *Manmade fibres are quick to dry and can be ideal for
  travelling when you do not want to take many nappies
  away with you.*

Can I buy preloved nappies and will they be any good?

Can I buy preloved nappies and will they be any good?

With the loss of independent high street stores and an increased drive in online shopping habits, getting to look and feel a particular brand or style of nappy is becoming ever more challenging.

Whilst in the long term, reusables can save you money compared to disposables, the initial outlay can be expensive and no one likes an expensive mistake. Do your research, ask for advice and consider preloved if you are not able to try before you buy.

SECOND HAND SAVIOURS

Buying preloved nappies will not only mitigate such a costly disaster, you are also contributing to a circular economy that in turn is better for people and planet. The very first nappies I bought were second hand. Like with any second hand purchase though, there are some telltale red flags to keep in mind when buying from an unknown source.

LOW QUALITY PHOTOGRAPHS

Us humans are tactile creatures. Take away the ability to touch or smell a product, we rely solely on our eyes to assess something's quality. If the images you see are dark, out of focus, or a 'stock' image used instead of the actual item you will be buying, be wary. An honest seller will photograph from multiple angles and actively highlight any flaws, like wear to Velcro fastenings, damaged fabric or worn elastics.

INCOMPLETE DESCRIPTIONS

Consumers are becoming more savvy every day around questioning what is in their products and where it comes from. Second hand should be no different. I love (am a sucker for) a story. I like to know why someone has decided to sell something they once chose to bring into their home. Is it simply too small? Are the leg elastics slack or have worn edges? Also expect to be told how long it has been used for, or with how many children, even if it is a guestimation. If they don't list this information, you can always try to ask. If the description box is incomplete, chances are it's not worth your time.

REOCCURING LISTINGS

Watch listings before making a purchase. You'll soon get a feel of how the real nappy community reacts to genuine, trustworthy sales. Posts that remain online with no interest can be telltale signs something is amiss. There may be a negative seller review linked to the account. Or it could simply be 'if you have nothing nice to say, don't say anything at all.' Gauging online marketplaces takes time and will help you not get caught up in the craze of '*sale ends soon, buy me now*.' A bargain isn't a bargain if you didn't need it in the first place.

COVETED PRINTS

I have yet to succumb to the thrawl of the new prints release dates. It also means I am not particularly knowledgable in what is a coveted design, and what is not. You may very well be the same. If a listing seems to be drawing unprecedented interest, this may be the reason - a limited edition on the second hand market. Also, just because someone has written 'rare print' in their item description does not necessarily mean this is the truth. Search online and if in doubt, contact the original manufacturer to find out if that print was indeed special and worthy of a higher price tag on the second hand market.

Whilst I have never heard of counterfeit cloth nappies being sold online, like with all desirable products, it is worth bearing this in mind. If it looks too good to be true, it probably is.

PREPARING NAPPIES

Whether or not you buy new or preloved reusable nappies, the first thing you will want to do is wash them. Preloved nappies that have been used more than five times will have reached their full absorbency - but don't be embarrassed to ask the seller how many times you think the nappy has been used. It may be that they bought it and decided they didn't like the print, so it has never been on a baby's bum before yours.

If you are buying new nappies, you need to improve their absorbency before letting baby wear them. Some manufacturers recommend soaking overnight in cold water. All I did is pop them in with a couple of loads of my regular washing, without bothering to let them dry between washes. Check the manufacturer's guidelines if you are unsure.

Reusable nappies
and the environment

Reusable nappies
and the environment

On average you can expect to change your baby's nappy six times a day. That's 42 nappies in a week. Or 180 in 30 days. Or how about, at best, 2,190 in one year. Think on until your child is ready to potty train sometime between two to three years of age. If using disposables, that is a lot of single use plastic that has to go somewhere.

400,000 TONNES OF WASTE A YEAR

In 2005 the Environment Agency reported that 2-3% of our household waste is estimated to be disposable nappies, approximately 400,000 tonnes of waste each year.[1]

When using disposables for my daughter back in 2016,

1 Environment Agency (2005). *Life Cycle Assessment of Disposable and Reusable Nappies in the UK.* P. 3

quite frankly I was unaware of the vast amount of plastics and adhesives contained in each disposable nappy. You may be the same, thinking the absorbency comes from natural materials like cotton or wood pulp (it doesn't). Disposable nappy manufacturers do not have to disclose a nappy's make up either online or on their (plastic) packaging.

500 YEARS TO BIODEGRADE

If you chose to dip your toe into the online cloth nappy community, it won't be long before you read the statistic that it is estimated it will take 500 years for one disposable nappy to biodegrade in landfill. Disposable nappies were invented sometime around the 1950s meaning, should the 500-year statistic be accurate, the very first disposable nappies to be used are still rotting in landfill now. They will be completely degraded by the year 2450. It is my understanding that this statistic is an estimate based on lab conditions of degradation on individual components of some of the materials found in disposable nappies. Clearly this isn't the whole picture.

The results of how long they really take to break down and what effect those chemicals have on the world as they slowly decompose will be determined well outside my lifetime - but not for our descendents. This is a risk I am no longer willing to take now I have done my research. And this is why. The Environment Agency's 2005 report concluded that "...for improving the environmental performance of disposable nappies [the focus] should be on the disposable nappy manufacturers and their suppliers whereas, with reusable nappies, it is the user who can achieve the most environmental gain through energy efficiency drives in the home."[2] I would assume this 'environmental performance' would include what happens and how long it takes for their product to reach the end of its life. That was 15 years ago and still there seems to be no definitive answer. Until disposable nappy companies are called on to do this research, I doubt we will ever know the truth.

But as the Environment Agency so eloquently put - with reusables, I have the power to maximise the environmental gain that comes hand in hand with cloth nappies. And gain the most, I shall.

MORE THAN JUST NAPPIES

In 2019 Zero Waste Europe published a report that offers, in a digestible way, a clear picture of what is going on in this environmental battle between three types of disposable and reusable products, including nappies. It breaks down the impact single use has on the environment from the processes undertaken in growing the natural resources required, to the greenhouse gases being emitted in their production, as well as accounting for the soiling caused by any leakages into the natural world. But this isn't with nappies alone.

---

2 Environment Agency (2005). *Life Cycle Assessment of Disposable and Reusable Nappies in the UK*. P. 121

WASTE GENERATION
'single-use baby nappies use 20 times more land for production of raw materials and require three times more energy to make than baby cloth nappies.'

WASTE PREVENTION
'a family that chooses reusable baby nappies can also save about 99% of the waste that would be generated by using single-use ones.'

'This potential waste reduction can be translated into [...] a reduction in the costs coming from removing waste from beaches and seas, as litter and sewage related debris would be reduced.'

FINANCIAL INCENTIVES
'the use of reusable nappies results in savings between €200 to €2,000 per family compared to single use ones. The saving increases if you take into account the fact that reusable baby nappies can be used by different siblings or bought second-hand.'

Zero Waste Europe (2019). *The Environmental & Economic Costs Of Single-Use Menstrual Products, Baby Nappies & Wet Wipes: Investigating the impact of these single-use items across Europe. P. 49 - 54*

Handfuls of plastic tampon applicators litter our beaches in swathes whilst plastic wet wipes continue to make new landmasses beneath our feet. There is a cost to all this - to public administrators dealing with the mess, and in turn the consumers who inadvertently incur the price hikes necessary to manage this waste. Knowing about it offers a vision for what our world could be if such simple changes, like reusable nappies and cloth wipes, are implemented on a larger scale.

The drumbeat of change is getting louder and louder every single day - I hear it tapping along with my heart's rhythm; I am guessing you do too.

WHAT ABOUT WIPES?

Baby wipes, including some so-called flushable wipes, contain plastics. In 2017, Water UK (the trade body representing all of the main water and sewerage companies in the United Kingdom) found that wipes made up around 93% of the materials blocking our sewers.[1] These plastics and synthetic fibres have to go somewhere. Friends of the Earth states: River-cleaning teams have found that the hundreds of thousands of wet wipes flushed down toilets in London have formed a new riverbed in the Thames. As in other rivers around the world too.[2] (How shameful.)

---

1 Water UK (2017). *Wipes in Sewer Blockage Study*. Report Ref. No. 21CDP.WS. P. 5
2 Friends of the Earth (2019). *Wet wipes: Keeping them out of our seas (and sewers)*. Available from: https://friendsoftheearth.uk/plastics/wet-wipes-keeping-them-out-our-seas-and-sewers. [Accessed May 2020]

BIODEGRADABLE AND COMPOSTABLE BABY WIPES

There are some single use wipes now marketed as biodegradable and/or compostable. If only it was that clear cut. The first question to ask is how is your household waste processed. If your council incinerates its general waste, your wipes won't go anywhere to biodegrade.

Compostable wipes are not considered safe to include in a home composting system because small scale composters do not reach high enough temperatures to kill off any pathogens or bacteria that may be found in human excreta, which spread disease. This is one reason they can also be incompatible with many municipality composting schemes. Another is that your council's start-to-end processing time (often around eight weeks) is not a long enough period for wipes to degrade, so you will be advised, like with biodegradable wipes, to put them in your general waste. If you are unsure, check.

Contact your local council before disposing of any single use wipes in your recycling, green waste or garden waste - wipes can be the cause of contamination resulting in whole batches of otherwise perfectly sound recyclables being sent to landfill or for incineration.

CLOTH WIPES

Cloth wipes are by far the easiest thing to use alongside cloth nappies. I roll mine inside my dirty nappies before putting the bundle in the nappy bucket. They get washed alongside my nappies. It really is simple. There is a wide range or reusable wipes on the market now, including those handmade by independent sellers. They are also very easy to make yourself - I have made some from my son's newborn baby towel which he quickly outgrew.

If you soak and store your cloth wipes damp, consider adding a few dashes of an essential oil to your airtight box. Tea Tree oil has natural antibacterial properties, whilst Lavender is known to calm and relax. I have heard some people like to soak wipes in Chamomile tea if their baby has nappy rash. If you do chose to use essential oils, be sure to always follow the guidelines.

Be proud of
yourself

Be proud of yourself

Like with so many ways of living a sustainable lifestyle, it doesn't have to be all or nothing - I may keep chickens but I am certainly not about to put a pig and a cow in my small suburban backyard so I can be fully self-sufficient (not yet anyway).

If you choose to use real nappies during the day but not at night, that's OK. If you need to stick to disposables for childcare settings, that's fine too. Do not beat yourself up if you don't cloth nappy full time; there is enough parent-induced guilt floating around to fill this planet twice over. But if full time works for you, then go for it.

So to end, I will say remember this - using one cloth nappy a day for two years adds up to saving 730 pieces of single use plastic from going to landfill or for incineration. That's a whole lot less 'stuff' floating unnecessarily around our world. Every reusable nappy helps. We are the ones securing a better future for our children.

Be proud of what you're doing.

You've got this.

A simple checklist for your cloth nappy journey

- »   1 nappy bucket, or a bucket with a secure lid

- »   2 mesh laundry bags

- »   2 wet bags *(one in use, one clean spare)*

- »   1 changing mat *(an extra for your changing bag is helpful)*

- »   20 reusable nappies for day time
  - a selection of the four nappy types will serve you well

- »   5 reusable nappies for night time
  - Two-part nappies are the most common for night

- »   Powder laundry detergent

EXTRAS

- »   30 reusable cloth wipes

- »   25 liners *(should you choose to use them)*

- »   3-5 vest extenders *(should you choose to use vests or bodysuits with popper fastenings at the crotch)*

- »   3-4 nippas *(should you use flat or prefold nappies)*

- »   A nappy sanitiser *(should you choose to wash at a lower temperature than 60°)*

Your
reusable nappies notes

A - Z of
reusable nappy brands*

A
Alvababy
Anavy

B
Baba+Boo
Baby BeeHinds™
Bambinex
Bambino Mio®
Bare and Boho
Bebeboo
Blueberry
Bright Bots
Bubblebubs
Bumkins®
Buttons Diapers

C
Charlie Banana®
Close Parent

D
Designer Bums

E
Easy Peasy Nappies
EcoNaps

Ecoposh®
Ella's House

F
FuzziBunz

G

H

I
Itti Bitti

J

K
Kanga Care®
Kings of my Castle

L
La Petite Ourse
Lil Joey®
Lil Learnerz®
Little Lamb

M

Mama Koala
Modern Cloth Nappies
Mother ease
MuslinZ
My Little Gumnut

N

Nappi Nippas

O

P

Petit Lulu
Petite Crown®
Popolini - organic parenting since 1991

Q

R

Real Nappies
Rumparooz®

S

Seedling Baby
Smart Bottoms

T

Thirsties
Tickle Tots

TotsBots

U, V

W

Wegreeco

X, Y, Z

*trading for a minimum of 12 months prior to May 2019.

A - Z of UK-based reusable nappy retailers[*]

A

B
Beaming Baby (beamingbaby.co.uk)

C, D

E
Earthlets (earthlets.com)

F
Fill your Pants (fill-your-pants.com)

G

H
HappiNappies (happinappies.co.uk)

I, J

K
KIDLY (kidly.co.uk)

L
Lizzie's Real Nappies (lizziesrealnappies.co.uk)

M
Mootooti (mootooti.com)

MerryGoRoundUK Ltd (merrygorounduk.co.uk)

N
Natural Baby Shower (naturalbabyshower.co.uk)
Naturally Baby (naturallybaby.co.uk)

O

P
Peace With The Wild (peacewiththewild.co.uk)

Q, R

S
Smallkind (smallkind.co.uk)

T
The Edinburgh Baby Company (edinburghbabyco.com)
The Nappy Gurus (thenappygurus.com)
The Nappy Lady (thenappylady.co.uk)
Tilly & Jasper (tillyandjasper.co.uk)
Twinkle Twinkle (twinkleontheweb.co.uk)

U, V, W, X

Y
Yes Bébé (yesbebe.co.uk)

Z

*trading either online or via online and in a shop registered under their trading name with Companies House, or include on their website the registered company number if different to their trading name, prior to May 2019

#clothmadesimple

For an introvert, stepping outside of their comfort zone is a challenge at the best of times. Actively turning the spotlight on themself is positively horrifying. If there was a supportive cloth nappy community on my doorstep, I may very well have said no when I was approached to join this online collective. But there wasn't. Clearly, the love of these little nappies (and a longing to belong) got me over my introversion.

We had a common goal of trying to make reusable nappies mainstream. Together this little community amplified each other's voices. In the process, we raised each other up. The 'team' gave me back the confidence I had lost in my abilities as a writer. *The Joy of Reusable Nappies* rumbled in the back of my mind and as more marvellous people started to share their own #clothmadesimple experiences on social media, it buoyed me on to carve out these words. You gave me back the love of writing I thought I had lost.

Undoubtedly I would not have had the courage to share this book with you without finally having found a community where I belong. Who knew a nappy could give so much more. To every single person who has shared their cloth journey online so far, I thank you. Together, we can share the joy of reusable nappies, one little square at a time.

You can view the back catalogue of our #clothmadesimple videos on my IGTV channel instagram.com/lauratweedale or on my website: lauratweedale.com/blog/nappy-chat

For more guidance and inspiration on keeping cloth simple, I encourage you to take a look at everyone's Instagram accounts, those featured in the videos and those who have made #clothmadesimple shares of their own.

I dare you not to smile.

Share some joy with the world
#joyofreusablenappies

Laura's acknowledgements

Firstly, thank you to my daughter and my son, for blessing me with their presence. You give me such remarkable joy. To my husband Mark, for supporting my dream of writing. You really are my soul mate. To my parents and family for always believing in me. You give me a strength like no other.

To my children's Guideparents Louise, Rivca, Richard and Kat, for showing my children that our differences provide the richness and diversity life has to offer.

To my #clothmadesimple friends Cecília, Chloe, Emma, Fafa, Laura-Jane, Louisa, Nicola and Amy, who coaxed me out of my introverted shell to take part in the project. Without your passion and enthusiasm for cloth nappies, the world would truly be a less colourful place.

To Jo from the High Peak NCT Nappy Library - your no-nonsense chat inspired me to write this book.

Finally, to every parent whose feet have walked this cloth nappy path before me, and those yet to come. I am grateful to you for doing something to secure a future for my children, and for all children, on this planet of ours.

Thank you.

Laura x

Index

"I alone cannot change the world, but I can cast a stone across the waters to create many ripples."

Mother Teresa

———————————

LAURA TWEEDALE

Laura Tweedale is a freelance writer and content creator based in Cheshire, England. She lives with her husband, their two children, one dog and three chickens. She has an MA in Creative Writing and BA (Hons) in Drama. Laura previously worked in marketing and communications for several charities and laterly, for one of the UK's largest universities.

After suffering from hyperemesis gravidarum whilst expecting her son, Laura was left with a hypersensitivity to synthetic fragrances that revolutionised how her family chose to live. She now writes regularly about the joy found in slow parenting and minimalist, sustainable living on her blog and for her regional community magazine.

She believes that everyone has the capacity to make a change to how they live to help secure a positive future for the planet. She hopes to galvanise others through her example.

LAURATWEEDALE.COM

Lightning Source UK Ltd.
Milton Keynes UK
UKHW020740110121
376656UK00007B/240